Twenty to Make

Sugar Sporties

Paula MacLeod

Search Press

First published in Great Britain 2012

Search Press Limited
Wellwood, North Farm Road,
Tunbridge Wells, Kent TN2 3DR

Text copyright © Paula MacLeod 2012

Photographs by Paul Bricknell at
Search Press Studios

Photographs and design copyright
© Search Press Ltd 2012

ISBN 978 1 84448 820 9

Suppliers
If you have difficulty in obtaining any of the
materials and equipment mentioned in this book,
then please visit the Search Press website for
details of suppliers: www.searchpress.com

Printed in Malaysia

Dedication

*I dedicate this book to the memory of my
mum Daphne, my dad Eric and to dear
nana Burrowes. The love you gave is ours
forever, the memories we will always
treasure. Gone but never forgotten.*

Contents

Introduction

All the models in this book have been made using modelling paste, a firm edible paste that enables the figures to hold their shape and makes modelling easier. Modelling paste is easily available ready-made from various sugarcraft outlets and online or you can easily make your own. Simply knead approximately 250g (8oz) of sugarpaste into a ball, make a well in the centre and add approximately half a teaspoon of gum tragacanth (or gum tex), also known as gum trac, or CMC into the centre. Fold the paste in over the top, knead the powder in thoroughly and leave it to firm up overnight. Using a little more or less gum will alter the consistency of the paste so experiment with the quantities until you achieve your preferred pliability.

Use sugar glue sparingly in all of the projects to stick the pieces of paste together. You can make your own by dropping two or three balls of modelling paste into 30ml (1fl oz) of cooled, boiled water and leaving it to dissolve. Edible glue works in a similar way to sugar glue and is readily available to buy, if you prefer. Apply with a small paintbrush.

To make it easy, I haven't weighed the paste or used a size guide, instead I have rolled my paste out between marzipan spacers of 1.3cm (½in) depth and used the 2.5cm (1in) circle cutter as a measuring tool e.g. a head might be half a circle or the arms one circle, and so on.

I have outlined how to make each basic shape that you will need for the projects on pages 6 and 7. You can model the hands without fingers to begin with and, as your confidence grows, mould the fingers, thumb and even fingernails! It is the same with the facial features – eyes can be marked on with piping tubes or drawn on with edible ink pens, but for more detail, cut the whites of the eyes out of paste with a piping tube. All the projects can be simplified by omitting some of the details, making this book ideal both for beginners and sugarcraft enthusiasts alike. The modelling techniques and projects provide a simplified, convenient and fuss-free approach to what I hope will be hours of fun and enjoyment, so be bold, be brave and and give it a go!

Basic shapes and tools

Preparing your paste Knead, and before rolling out your paste, sprinkle your work surface with a little icing sugar to stop it sticking. Place your spacers either side of your paste and roll your rolling pin over the surface. The spacers will help you to achieve an even thickness. You can then cut out your shapes using various cutters.

Ball To make a ball, place the paste between the palms of your hands and roll using a circular motion.

Oval Roll the ball to and fro on your work surface to make an oval shape.

Pear Roll the oval into a pear shape by using the edge of your palms to make one end thinner than the other.

Arms and legs Use your fingers to lengthen an oval; place it on your work surface and roll it back and forth into a sausage shape. Use a smoother to remove any finger marks, but do not squash. This shape can then be used to make arms and legs and can be cut in half.

Joints Place your little finger on the areas where the wrists and elbows or ankles and knees will be and and roll back and forth on the work surface. This will thin the paste to define these areas. Pinch to create bends.

Hands Work on the hands in pairs with thumbs to the inside. You can make the simple, round hands, mitten-shaped hands or hands with fingers. Roll a large pea-sized amount of paste into a ball, cut it in half and roll it into a cone shape for each hand. To make round hands define the wrist and flatten the palm slightly. For mitten-shaped hands, use a craft knife to cut out a small triangle from the round hand to make a thumb. Round off the sharp edges with a scriber. To make fingers, bend the thumb away from the palm slightly, divide the palm with a central cut and then divide the remaining paste on each side with another cut. Separate each finger using a scriber and round off each finger by pinching carefully. Mark on the fingernails using a no. 3 piping tube or a drinking straw used at an angle.

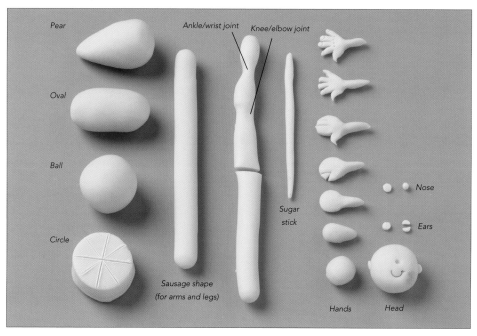

Pear · Oval · Ball · Circle · Ankle/wrist joint · Knee/elbow joint · Sugar stick · Sausage shape (for arms and legs) · Nose · Ears · Hands · Head

Head Use the 2.5cm (1in) circle cutter to cut out the number of circles of paste the project requires and roll into a ball. Using a mini ball tool, approximately in the centre of the ball, make a recess for the nose. Push the tool lightly into the paste ball. To add colour to the cheeks, apply edible dust sparingly with a very small soft paintbrush; remove the excess on a piece of kitchen paper first.

Mouth Push a mini scallop tool into the paste to make a smile or frown and use a craft knife to add the corners of the mouth.

Nose Roll out some paste thinly and use no. 3 or 4 piping tubes to cut out a circle. Roll into a ball and secure into the recess in the centre of the head, using sugar glue.

Ears Roll out some paste thinly and use no. 3 or 4 piping tubes to cut out a circle. Roll it into a ball and cut it in half to make two ears. Attach one at each side of the head, using sugar glue.

Sugar sticks Leftover paste can be made into sugar sticks when rolled to different sizes and thicknesses. Use in any of the projects to give extra strength to the figures.

Tools

Marzipan/plastic spacers, 1.3cm (½in) depth

Square cutter, 4cm (1½in)

Piping tubes no. 3, 4, 17

Smoother

Non-stick rolling pin

Foam pad

Circle and round/wavy cutters, 1.3cm (½in), 2.5cm (1in), 3cm (1¼in), 4.5cm (1¾in), 5.7cm (2¼in),7cm (2¾in).

Oval/fluted oval cutter 12.7cm (5in)

Blossom plunger, 2.5cm (1in)

Blossom plunger, 1cm (½in)

Cocktail sticks

Mini ball tool

Mini scallop tool

Small paintbrush

Scriber

Scissors

Bulbous cone tool

Ball tool/mini ball tool

Leaf veining tool

Craft knife

Other tools:
Drinking straws
Disposable piping bags
Food bags
Palette knife
Tweezers
Cutting wheel
Blade tool
Quilting tool/stitch wheel

Football

Materials:

Modelling paste: flesh, white, red, brown, black

Chocolate football or football cake decoration

Sugar glue

Edible ink pen in black or brown

Tools:

Marzipan/plastic spacers, 1.3cm (½in) depth

Non-stick rolling pin

Circle cutter, 2.5cm (1in)

Square cutter, 4cm (1½in)

Smoother

Bulbous cone tool

Cutting wheel

Mini scallop tool

Ball tool/mini ball tool

Piping tube no. 3

Blossom plunger, 1cm (⅜in)

Food bag

Craft knife

Scriber

Leaf veining tool

Small paintbrush

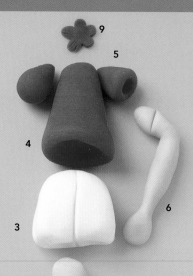

Instructions:

1 To make the socks, roll out some white modelling paste and cut out two squares with the 4cm (1½in) cutter. Fold over one edge on each to make a turnover. Place both in a food bag.

2 For the legs, cut out two circles of the flesh-coloured paste. Roll each into a long sausage shape about 10cm (4in) long, one for each leg (see page 6). Secure a sock to the end of each leg and bend into a kneeling position, moulding the top for a waist.

3 For the shorts, roll two circles of white paste into an oval shape, flatten slightly with the smoother and shape to a rectangle with rounded edges. Hollow out the bottom end of the shorts slightly with the bulbous cone tool, run a cutting wheel down the middle of the shorts for a seam and secure to the tops of the legs (waist end) with sugar glue.

4 To make the football shirt, roll two circles of red paste into a pear shape. Push your thumb into the wide end to make a hollow and secure to the shorts.

5 For each shirt sleeve, roll a quarter of a circle into a cone shape. Indent the wide end with the ball tool (so that it will be easier to attach to the arm) and secure to each side of the top of the shirt (pointed end at the top).

6 Use half a circle of flesh-coloured modelling paste per arm and follow the instructions on page 6. Attach to the sleeves with sugar glue.

7 Use an eighth of a circle of black paste per shoe and roll into an oval shape. Mark with the cutting wheel to define the heel and sole. Position at the base of each leg.

8 For the head, use half a circle of flesh-coloured paste and follow the instructions on page 7. Attach to the top of the shirt with sugar glue. For the mouth, ears and nose follow the instructions on page 7. Draw on the eyes and eyebrows with the edible ink pen. Alternatively, for the eyes, roll out some white paste, thinly, and using a no. 3 piping tube cut out two very small circles and sugar glue them on to the head. Leave to dry before marking on the pupils with an edible ink pen.

9 For the hair, roll out a small amount of brown paste and cut out a flower shape with the 1cm (⅜in) blossom plunger. Add texture using the leaf veining tool and secure it to the top of the head with sugar glue.

Back of the Net

Make your footballer a member of the team you support by changing the colour of his or her shirt. Bend the limbs in different positions to put your player in some dynamic, goal-scoring poses and recreate a scene on your cake. Here I have used drinking straws for the goal posts and coconut dyed green with food colouring for the grass.

Basketball

Materials:

Modelling paste: flesh, blue, white, orange, beige

Edible ink pen in black

Edible red dust

Pastillage or lollipop sticks

Sugar glue

Buttercream/frosting

Tools:

Marzipan/plastic spacers, 1.3cm (½in) depth

Circle cutter, 2.5cm (1in)

Non-stick rolling pin

Craft knife

Leaf veining tool

Mini scallop tool

Blossom cutter, 2.5cm (1in)

Piping tube no. 3 or 4

Smoother

Ball tool/mini ball tool

Small paintbrush

Kitchen paper

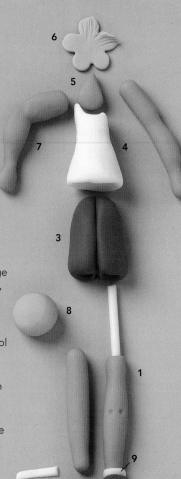

Instructions:

1 For the lower legs, cut out one circle of flesh-coloured paste, roll it into a 10cm (4in) long sausage shape and cut it in half to give you two lower legs. Using the mini ball tool, mark two indentations on to each knee cap.

2 For the feet, roll a large pea-sized ball of blue paste into an oval shape, position at the base of each leg and push a pastillage or long lollipop stick through both the top and base of each leg, including the shoes.

3 For the shorts, take one and a half circles of blue paste and roll it into an oval shape, then a rectangle with rounded edges. Hollow out the bottom end of the shorts slightly with the ball tool and mark on the central line with the leaf veining tool.

4 For the vest, roll one circle of white paste into an oval, push your thumb into the base to hollow it out slightly and make each shoulder strap by pinching the paste on each side at the top between a finger and thumb. Secure with glue above the shorts.

5 For the chest, take an eighth of a circle of flesh-coloured paste and roll it into a ball, then into a triangular shape with rounded edges. Ease it into the top of the vest and pinch away any excess paste.

6 For the head, take a circle of flesh-coloured paste and follow the instructions on page 7. Use the comb end of a mini scallop tool to mark on the mouth. For the ears and nose follow the instructions on page 7. When dry draw on the eyes and eyebrows with the edible ink pen. For the hair, roll out some beige paste and use the 2.5cm (1in) blossom cutter to cut out the shape. Smooth the edges with a finger to thin them slightly and add texture with the leaf veining tool. Secure to the head with sugar glue with the hair lifting.

7 To make the arms, follow the instructions on page 6 and secure to the body with a little sugar glue. Lay the figure on its back in your chosen pose and leave to dry overnight.

8 For the basketball, take one circle of orange paste and cut it in half. Roll it into a ball and leave it to dry before using an edible ink pen to mark on the lines. Attach it to the head and hands with a little buttercream.

9 For the socks, use a little rolled-out white paste cut into thin strips and secure above each shoe with sugar glue.

Shoot Some Hoops

The pressure is on for this plucky player – just look at the concentration on his face as he prepares to score a basket!

Beach Volleyball

Materials:

Modelling paste: flesh, pink, white, black, plus any three colours of your choice for the ball

Edible ink pens in black and blue

Edible red dust

Pastillage or lollipop sticks

Sugar glue

Tools:

Marzipan/plastic spacers, 1.3cm (½in) depth

Non-stick rolling pin

Craft knife

Circle cutter, 2.5cm (1in)

Ball tool

Mini ball tool

Mini scallop tool

Smoother

Piping tube no. 3

Small paintbrush

Kitchen paper

Instructions:

1 For the legs, take one flesh-coloured circle of paste, cut it in half and roll each half into a sausage shape 6.5cm (2½in) long. Insert a pastillage or lollipop stick into the top and the bottom of each leg. Using the mini ball tool, mark two indentations on to the knee cap. There are no feet to model for this project.

2 For the body, use one circle of pink paste and roll it into an oval shape. Indent the leg and arm sockets with the ball tool.

3 For the arms, take one circle of flesh-coloured paste, cut it in half and follow the instructions on page 6. Insert a pastillage stick through the length of each arm to strengthen if necessary.

4 For the head, take a circle of flesh-coloured paste and follow the instructions on page 6. For the nose and mouth also follow the instructions on page 7 and draw on the eyes with the black edible ink pen. Alternatively, for the eyes, roll out some white paste, thinly, and using a no. 3 piping tube, cut out two very small circles and sugar glue them on to the head. Leave to dry before marking on the pupil with an edible ink pen.

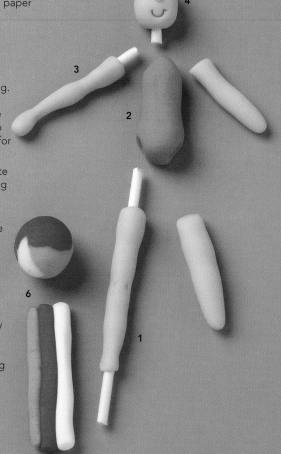

5 To make the hair, take a small amount of black paste and model into teardrop shapes. Stick these randomly on the head with sugar glue, with some sticking up at various angles for movement. Leave the model to dry flat at least overnight.

6 To make the volleyball, take three different colours of leftover paste, roll them to size between the spacers and cut out one circle of each colour. Roll each circle into a sausage shape and roll them altogether into a ball. Leave to dry overnight. Your volleyball players will stand up if you insert the lollipop sticks into a cake. Decorate the cake with brown sugar to give the impression of a sandy beach.

Go Girls!

Capturing the essence of sun, fun and games on the beach, these girls love to volley the day away!

Baseball

Tools:

Non-stick rolling pin

Marzipan/plastic spacers, 1.3cm (½in) depth

Circle cutter, 2.5cm (1in)

Piping tube no. 3 or 4

Smoother

Craft knife

Scriber

Ball tool/mini ball tool

Square cutter, 4cm (1½in)

Kitchen paper

Cutting wheel

Small paintbrush

Materials:

Modelling paste in the following colours: white, brown, blue, black

Sugar glue

Liquorice strand

Instructions:

1 For the upper body, take one and a half circles of white paste and roll into a pear shape. Roll the wide end into a 'T' shape to make sleeves. Push your thumb up into the thinner, waist end to form a hollow. Make a recess for each arm with a ball tool, into each sleeve. Bend the shoulders upwards slightly and support the model in this position with kitchen paper as you leave it to dry a little.

2 For the legs, use two circles of white paste and, following the instructions on page 6, roll to a total length of 15cm (6in) and cut in half. Bend each leg in half where the knee would be. Secure into the hollow of the upper body (waist end) with sugar glue.

3 Secure a strip of liquorice around the player's middle to form a belt. Trim it to fit.

4 For the arms, use a quarter of a circle of brown paste for each, following the instructions on page 6. Secure each one into the slightly hollowed sleeves with a little sugar glue, positioning them as if he's just dropped the bat or is ready to catch the ball.

5 For the head, roll half a circle of brown paste into a ball and follow the instructions on page 7, then cut the head in half. Make the nose following the instructions on page 7 and mark on the mouth with the mini ball tool. For the hat take half a circle of blue paste, roll it into a ball and cut it in half and secure to the head. Roll out the remaining blue paste and cut out a circle 2.5cm (1in) for the brim. Cut this circle in half and secure it to the hat with sugar glue.

6 For the bat, roll half a circle of brown paste into a tapered sausage shape and shape with your fingers. Use a cutting wheel to texture a wood grain effect on to the surface.

7 Roll out some black paste and cut out a square using the 4cm (1½in) cutter. From this square, use the cutter to cut out a rectangular strip and wrap it around the thin end of the bat to make the handle. Place the bat to one side or secure to the hand with sugar glue.

8 For the feet, roll a large pea-sized ball of blue paste for each shoe into an oval shape, flatten slightly and run a cutting wheel around its edge to look like a sole. Position at the base of each leg and secure with sugar glue.

Home Run
First base...second base...create a memorable sporting moment on your cake with this American favourite.

American Football

Tools:

Marzipan/plastic spacers, 1.3cm (½in) depth

Non-stick rolling pin

Circle cutter, 2.5cm (1in)

Craft knife

Smoother

Scriber

Piping tube no. 3 or drinking straw

Ball tool

Cutting wheel

Leaf veining tool

Small paintbrush

Materials:

Modelling paste: pale brown, white, pale blue, dark brown

Sugar glue

Instructions:

1 For the upper legs, measure out one circle of white paste per leg. Roll each circle into a tapered sausage shape measuring 4cm (1½in). Lay each side by side and pinch together at the wide end to form buttocks. Use the leaf veining tool to give the impression of creases on the footballer's trousers.

2 Trim the other tapered end to a straight edge using the craft knife.

3 For the lower leg, use a quarter of a circle of pale blue paste and roll into a tapered sausage shape approximately 2.5cm (1in) long, with one end slightly wider than the other.

4 Trim the wider end to a straight edge, texture with the narrow end of a leaf veining tool as before and secure to the upper leg with a little sugar glue.

5 Make a shoe by rolling an eighth of a blue circle into an oval, flatten slightly and run a cutting wheel around its edge to look like a sole.

6 For the upper body, roll two blue circles into a pear shape 3cm (1¼in) long. Roll the wide end into a 'T' shape. Push your thumb up into the thinner, waist end to form a hollow. Make a recess for each arm with the large end of a ball tool.

7 For the arms, use three-quarters of a circle of pale brown paste, divide it in half and follow the instructions on page 6.

8 Secure the arms in position with sugar glue. Flatten a pea-sized amount of white paste with a rolling pin and trim to a rectangle. Use to cover the join between the arm and the shirt.

9 For the head, use half a circle of pale brown paste and roll it into a ball.

10 For the hair, roll a large pea-sized amount of dark brown paste into a sausage shape and add lots of texture using the leaf veining tool. Secure to the back of the head with a little sugar glue.

11 To make the helmet, roll one circle of blue paste into a ball, flatten slightly so that it measures approximately 4cm (1½in) across. Attach it to the head, ensuring it covers the join of the hair.

It's a Touchdown!

Change the colours of your player's kit and add a paste ball for them to hold. For someone's birthday you could even write their name and age on the back of the player's shirt using an edible ink pen to make it extra personal.

Running

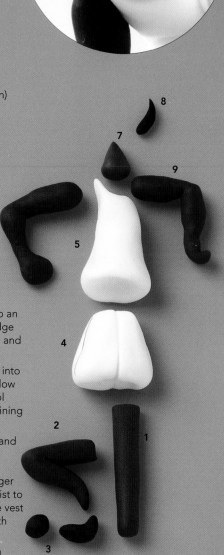

Materials:

Modelling paste: white, brown, black

Edible ink pens in black and blue

Pastillage or lollipop sticks

Sugar glue

Tools:

Marzipan/plastic spacers, 1.3cm (½in) depth

Non-stick rolling pin

Craft knife

Smoother

Scriber

Ball tool/mini ball tool

Mini scallop tool

Circle cutter, 2.5cm (1in)

Piping tube no. 3 or 4

Leaf veining tool

Small paintbrush

Cutting wheel

Instructions:

1 For the legs, roll one circle of brown paste into a long sausage shape (see page 6), measuring 11.5cm (4½in) long and cut it in half (don't add feet).

2 Bend each leg in half and pinch at the knee between your finger and thumb to define the knee joint. Secure both legs together at the top with a little sugar glue.

3 For each shoe, roll an eighth of a black paste circle into an oval, flatten slightly and run a cutting wheel around its edge to look like a sole. Secure under each leg with sugar glue and leave to dry overnight.

4 For the shorts, take one circle of white paste and roll it into an oval shape, then a rectangle with rounded edges. Hollow out the bottom end of the shorts slightly with the ball tool (for the legs) and mark on the central line with the leaf veining tool. Bend into the runner's starting position.

5 For the vest, take one and a half circles of white paste and roll into an oval shape. Push your thumb up into the base to hollow it out slightly and make each shoulder strap by pinching the paste on each side at the top between a finger and thumb. Attach it on to the shorts and bend at the waist to pose the figure. Push a pastillage or lollipop stick into the vest to help keep the head from falling off. Secure the vest with sugar glue on top of the shorts.

6 Using the blue edible ink pen, add a stripe detail down each side of the shorts when they are dry.

7 For the chest, take an eighth of a circle of brown paste and roll it into a ball, then into a triangular shape with rounded edges. Ease it into the top of the vest and pinch away any excess paste.

8 For the head, take a circle of brown paste and follow the instructions on page 7. For the nose and ears, follow the instructions on page 7 and draw on the eyes and eyebrows with the black edible ink pen. Use a mini scallop tool for the mouth. To make the hair, roll three very small teardrops of black paste between your fingers and secure them to the top of the head with sugar glue.

9 To make the arms, take one circle of brown paste and model following the directions on page 6. Pinch each arm at the elbow between your finger and thumb to define the joint and leave the hands mitten-shaped. Attach to either side of the vest at the straps.

On Your Marks

Looking tense on their starting blocks these two athletes prepare for their sprint. Make a running track like this one out of colourful sprinkles and liquorice strands.

Long Jump

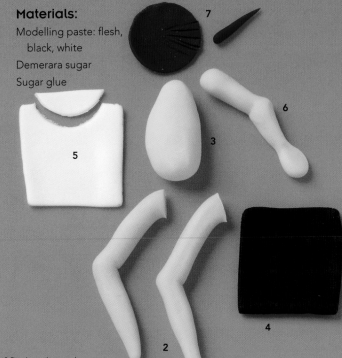

7

6

3

5

4

2

Tools:

Marzipan/plastic spacers,
  1.3cm (½in) depth

Non-stick rolling pin

Craft knife

Square cutter, 4cm (1½in)

Circle cutter, 2.5cm (1in)

Piping tube no. 3 or 4

Cutting wheel

Kitchen paper

Food bag

Mini scallop tool

Small paintbrush

Smoother

Materials:

Modelling paste: flesh,
  black, white

Demerara sugar

Sugar glue

Instructions:

1 For the legs, use one circle of flesh-coloured paste.
Roll to a sausage shape, tapered at each end, 11.5cm (4½in) long and
follow the instructions on page 6. No feet are required for this project.

2 Cut the sausage in half to make two legs and pinch each one slightly at the
knee between your finger and thumb. Position the bended legs into upside
down 'V' shapes. A little rolled-up kitchen paper will help them to maintain the
position while drying.

3 For the body, take one circle of flesh paste and roll into an oval shape,
following the directions on page 6. Secure on to the legs
with sugar glue with the narrowest point upwards.

4 To make the shorts, roll out some black modelling paste
quite thinly and use the 4cm (1½in) square cutter to cut out
two shapes. Drape one black square over the front and one
over the back of the legs and body. Trim to fit and smooth
with your finger to disguise the join.

5 For the vest, roll out some white paste quite thinly and
cut out one square using the same cutter. Cut this square in
half using the cutting wheel or the square cutter. Remove
a semi-circle from one side of each square using the 2.5cm
(1in) circle cutter and discard. This shapes the paste into a
vest with straps. Store in a food bag.

6 For the arms, use half a circle of flesh-coloured paste and follow the instructions on page 6. Roll the paste to a sausage shape, 9.5cm (3¾in) long and then cut it in half. There is no need to shape hands for this project as these will be buried in the sand. Remove the vest pieces from the food bag and secure both sides to the body with sugar glue, leaving enough space for the arms to be secured. Join the straps of the vest together at the shoulders. Attach both arms in place with a little sugar glue.

7 For the head, take half a circle of flesh-coloured paste and follow the instructions on page 7. Add the nose and mouth and secure to the body with sugar glue. Mark on the eyes with the mini scallop tool. For the hair, cut out some brown paste using the 2.5cm (1in) circle cutter then add texture with the cutting wheel. Secure it to the head and make a few small teardrop shapes of paste for a fringe, and a larger teardrop shape for a ponytail and bend into position randomly on the head for movement. Place your sugar model into demerara sugar to give the impression she has just landed in the long jump sandpit.

Sandy Landing

After a long run up and launching themselves into the air, these two make a sugary, sandy landing, but by the looks on their faces they're not too happy with the result! Turn those frowns upside-down by using the mini scallop tool the other way up for the mouths.

Gymnastics

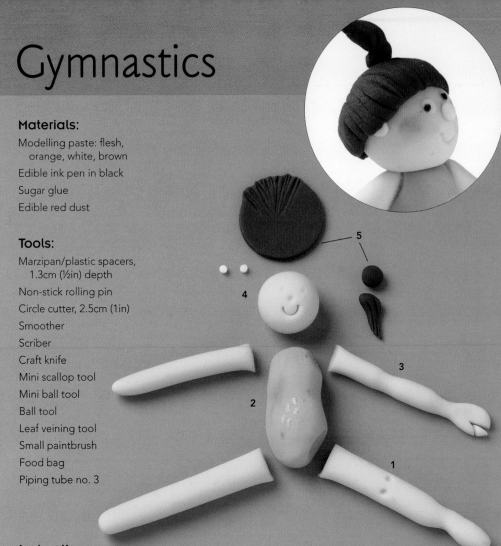

Materials:

Modelling paste: flesh,
  orange, white, brown
Edible ink pen in black
Sugar glue
Edible red dust

Tools:

Marzipan/plastic spacers,
  1.3cm (½in) depth
Non-stick rolling pin
Circle cutter, 2.5cm (1in)
Smoother
Scriber
Craft knife
Mini scallop tool
Mini ball tool
Ball tool
Leaf veining tool
Small paintbrush
Food bag
Piping tube no. 3

Instructions:

1 For the legs, take one circle of flesh-coloured paste, roll it into
a ball and then a sausage shape about 11.5cm (4½in) long and
cut it in half (follow the instructions on page 6). Bend to an 'L'
shape to make the foot and indent the knee cap twice with a ball
tool to define the joint.

2 For the body, take one circle of orange paste and roll it into
an oval shape. Indent the leg and arm sockets with the large end
of the ball tool, and attach the legs using sugar glue by pushing
them into the prepared sockets.

3 For the arms, take one circle of flesh-coloured paste and cut
it in half (put the other half in a food bag). Roll it into a sausage
shape, cut it in half and follow the directions on page 6. Position
the arms to suit and secure into the prepared sockets with
sugar glue.

4 For the head, take half a circle of flesh-coloured paste and follow the instructions on page 7. Make the nose, mouth and ears (see page 7). To make the eyes, roll out some white paste thinly and, using a no. 3 piping tube, cut out two circles and sugar glue them on to the head. Leave to dry before marking on the pupil with an edible ink pen.

5 For the hair, roll out some brown paste thinly, and cut out a 2.5cm (1in) circle with the cutter. Add texture with the leaf veining tool and secure to the head with sugar glue. Indent a small hollow on the centre-back of the head using a mini ball tool – this will stop the ponytail from falling off. Make a small teardrop shape of brown paste for the ponytail and bend it into position randomly on the head for movement.

Take to the Floor

Showing off just how flexible modelling paste can be, these gymnasts make a colourful duo on the mats. Try varying the flesh colour, modelling a different colour leotard and bending the limbs into ever more challenging positions! These would make great yoga poses too.

Judo

Materials:

Modelling paste: white, flesh, brown

Sugar glue

Liquorice strand

Tools:

Marzipan/plastic spacers, 1.3cm (½in) depth

Non-stick rolling pin

Circle cutter, 2.5cm (1in)

Smoother

Cutting wheel

Blossom plunger, 1cm (⅜in)

Small paintbrush

Piping tube no. 3 or 4

Craft knife

Scriber

Ball tool

Mini ball tool

Mini scallop tool

Leaf veining tool

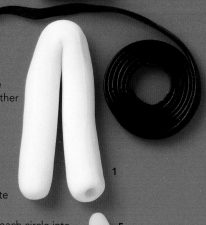

Instructions:

1 For the legs, cut out four circles of white paste and roll into a sausage shape (following the instructions on page 6) approximately 15cm (6in) long, and fold in half. Indent the foot end of each leg with the ball tool; bend one of the legs.

2 To make the body, roll two and a half circles of white paste into an oval shape, flatten slightly with the smoother and cut out a triangle of paste at the neck area and remove. Push your thumb up into the paste at the opposite end to create a slight hollow. Use a cutting wheel to mark the details on the clothing. Tie a strand of liquorice around the waist to make a belt.

3 For the chest, cut out a quarter of a circle of flesh-coloured paste and ease it into place on the white paste body. Secure with sugar glue.

4 For each arm, cut out one circle of white paste. Roll each circle into a sausage shape approximately 4cm (1½in) long, but with one end wider than the other. Indent the wider end of each arm with the ball tool where the hands will be attached.

5 To make the hands, use flesh-coloured paste and follow the instructions on page 6. To make the feet, take a large pea-sized ball of flesh-coloured paste for each foot and roll them into oval shapes. Attach the hands and feet in position with sugar glue.

6 For the head, take half a circle of flesh-coloured paste and follow the instructions on page 7. Use a mini ball tool to mark on the mouth and a mini scallop tool for the closed eyes. Make the ears and nose according to page 7.

7 For the hair, roll out some brown paste thinly, and cut out a blossom shape using the 1cm (⅜in) blossom plunger. Add texture using the leaf veining tool and secure it to the top of the head with sugar glue.

Black Belt

If you know someone who is truly spectacular at martial arts, this cake topper will work a treat. Simply change the belt to match their skill level using different coloured liquorice or sweet strands.

Windsurfing

Materials:

Pale blue sugarpaste,
   250g (8oz)

Modelling paste: orange, pale
   brown, black, bright yellow

White buttercream/frosting

Rice paper

Red edible dust

Edible lustre spray in blue

Piping gel

Food colouring in blue

Lollipop sticks

Sugar glue

Tools:

Marzipan/plastic spacers,
   1.3cm (½in) depth

Non-stick rolling pin

Oval/fluted oval cutter,
   12.7cm (5in)

Circle cutter, 2.5cm (1in)

Square cutter, 4cm (1½in)

Craft knife

Scriber

Smoother

Mini scallop tool

Mini ball tool

Piping tubes no. 3 or 4, 17

Small paintbrush

Kitchen paper

Leaf veining tool

Cutting wheel

Instructions:

1 Roll out the pale blue sugarpaste and cut out the
surfboard using the 12.7cm (5in) oval cutter and the base
using the 12.7cm (5in) fluted oval cutter. Spray the fluted
oval base with edible lustre spray in blue. When it has
dried, secure the surfboard to the base with
a little buttercream. Using the template, cut out
a sail from rice paper.

2 For the legs, cut out two circles of pale brown
paste; follow the instructions on page 6 and roll
them into a sausage shape, 16.5cm (6½in) long.

*The sail template is shown
half of actual size.
Enlarge 200% on
a photocopier.*

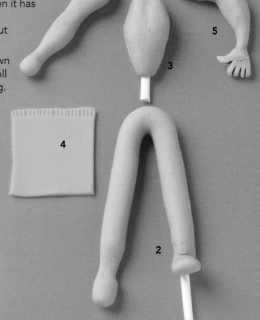

Bend the sausage in half to form two legs and insert a lollipop stick up through each ankle, leaving a little of the stick exposed at the end.

3 For the body, take one circle of pale brown paste and roll it into an oval shape, and then to a slight point for the waist. Add detail to the chest using the flat end of a leaf veining tool and secure to the legs, using sugar glue. Use a lollipop stick for reinforcement if necessary.

4 To make the shorts, roll out some orange paste quite thinly and cut out two squares using the 4cm (1½in) cutter. Use the straight comb edge of the mini scallop tool to mark a design around the waistband on each square. Secure one square to the front of your model and the other to the back to make up the shorts. Trim away any excess paste and smooth with your finger to neaten.

5 For the arms, take one circle of pale brown paste and roll it into a long sausage shape about 9.5cm (3¾in) long and cut it in half. Follow the instructions on page 6 to make the arms and the hands. Point the thumb upwards and curl the fingers inwards on one hand. For the other arm, position it away from the body in a waving position or ready to hold the sail and secure the arms to the body with sugar glue. Use kitchen paper to support the arms in position while they dry.

6 For the head, use half of a circle of pale brown paste and follow the instructions on page 7. Make sunglasses by rolling out a very small amount of black paste and cutting out two circles using a no.17 piping tube. Remove the top edge of each circle with a cutting wheel and secure each one either side of the nose.

7 Mould a few small teardrop-shaped pieces of bright yellow paste for the hair and position these randomly on the head for movement. When the figure is dry, secure the sail to the blue board with buttercream, anchoring it at the edges with a little leftover paste to hold it as it dries. When it is dry, position your windsurfer on the board, press the lollipop sticks from his feet into the board, and secure with a little buttercream. Use kitchen paper to keep him upright until everything has dried fully.

8 Add on some piping gel coloured blue with food colouring around the surfboard for waves.

Catch the Wave

This surf dude is ready to ride those waves! With his tanned skin, golden hair, shades and shorts, he certainly looks the part! Perfect for a sporty sun-worshipper!

Sailing

Materials:

White sugarpaste, 340g (12oz)

Modelling paste: blue, white, orange, pale brown, yellow

Sugar glue

Rice paper

Edible ink pen in blue

Edible red dust

Tools:

Marzipan/plastic spacers, 1.3cm (½in) depth

Non-stick rolling pin

Circle cutter, 2.5cm (1in)

Oval cutter, 12.7cm (5in)

Square cutter, 4cm (1½in)

Cutting wheel

Leaf veining tool

Craft knife

Smoother

Scriber

Ball tool

Mini ball tool

Scissors

Ruler

Hole punch

Cookie stick

Small paintbrush

Piping tube no. 3 or 4

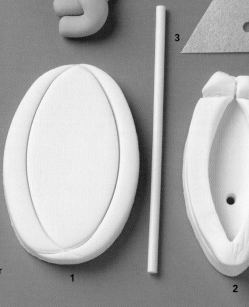

Instructions:

1 To make the boat, roll out some white sugarpaste and cut out an oval using the 12.7cm (5in) cutter. Re-cut the shape to make it more of a boat shape with pointed ends using the cutter (see right).

2 Roll some white sugarpaste into a sausage shape, flatten slightly to the depth of the spacers and add to the outside edge of the boat. Trim off any excess paste with a craft knife so that it fits the size of the boat, making sure the edges are neat. Use the cutting wheel to create a wood grain effect by dragging through the paste. Shape the front of the boat to more of a point than the back by smoothing the paste between your finger and thumb.

3 For the sail, use an edible ink pen to draw a triangle on to the sheet of rice paper measuring 10cm (4in) by 6.5cm (2½in) and cut out with some scissors. Use the hole punch to make two holes, one near the top and one near the bottom of the triangle. Thread the cookie stick through the holes, dip the end in sugar glue and push your sail into the inside of the boat towards the front.

4 For the legs, take two circles of blue paste, roll them into a ball and then make a sausage shape of paste measuring approximately 12.5cm (5in) long. Bend it in half, then bend one half (one leg) over the other and position at the side of the boat.

5 For the body, cut out one circle of blue paste, roll it into an oval shape and mark on the zip by using the sharp end of the leaf veining tool.

6 For the arms, use one circle of blue paste and roll it to a length of 6.5cm (2½in). Cut it in half, indent each end with the ball tool for the hands and add texture with a leaf veining tool. Cut across the top of each arm ready to attach them to the body.

7 For the life jacket, use the 4cm (1½in) square cutter and orange paste and make in the same way as the vest on page 20. Secure the life jacket to the body with sugar glue.

8 To make the hands, take a large pea-sized amount of pale brown modelling paste and follow the instructions on pages 6–7. Secure them to the ends of the arms with sugar glue and secure one hand so that it rests on the edge of the boat and the other holding the sail.

9 Cut out half a circle of brown modelling paste to make the head, and follow the instructions on page 7. Add on the ears, nose and mouth (page 7). Make the eyes in the same way as for the footballer on page 9. Secure the head to the body with sugar glue.

10 Create the hair by rolling small balls of yellow modelling paste into teardrop shapes. Secure them to the head, positioning them randomly, with sugar glue.

Sail Away

Use some edible lustre spray in blue on your rice paper sail to give it some movement – the spray makes it curl as if in the wind. Then your sailor's boat is ready to sail the sugary seas. For keen sailors, give your boat a name using an edible ink pen.

Canoeing

Tools:

Marzipan/plastic
  spacers, 1.3cm
  (½in) depth

Non-stick rolling pin

Circle cutter,
  2.5cm (1in)

Oval cutter,
  12.7cm (5in)

Square cutter,
  4cm (1½in)

Small paintbrush

Leaf veining tool

Kitchen paper

Craft knife

Ball tool/mini ball tool

Mini scallop tool

Smoother

Scriber

Piping tube no. 3 or 4

Materials:

Yellow sugarpaste,
  250g (8oz)

Modelling paste:
  green, beige,
  orange, brown,
  white

Edible ink pens in
  blue and brown

Rice paper

Buttercream/frosting

Edible lustre spray
  in pearl

Sugar stick (optional)

Sugar glue

Food colouring in
  brown

Lollipop stick

Instructions:

1 For the boat, roll out some yellow
sugarpaste and cut out an oval using the
12.7cm (5in) cutter. Re-cut the shape to give it more pointed
ends using the cutter, as pictured on this page. Use the 2.5cm
(1in) circle cutter to remove the centre, where your canoeist
will sit.

2 Paint the lollipop stick with brown food colouring and leave it to dry.

3 For the body, use one circle of green paste, shape it into an oval and mark on
the zip by using the sharp end of the leaf veining tool.

4 Roll out two circles of orange paste and cut out two squares with the 4cm (1½in)
cutter. Make the life jacket in the same way as the vest on page 20 and secure to
the body.

5 To make the head, use one circle of beige paste and follow the instructions on page 7. Make the nose and mouth as on page 7, and make the eyes in the same way as for the footballer on page 9. Make the hair using brown paste, in the same way as for the windsurfer on page 27. Add a small ball of paste for the neck before attaching the head with sugar glue. Insert a sugar stick through the body, neck and head to secure if necessary.

6 For the arms, use one circle of green paste and roll it to a length of 6.5cm (2½in). Cut it in half, indent each end with the ball tool where the hands will be secured and add texture with a leaf veining tool. Trim the top of each arm (pictured opposite) ready to attach them to the body.

7 For the hands, roll a large pea-sized ball of beige paste and divide it in half. Follow the instructions on pages 6–7. Wrap the hands around the lollipop stick, secure with sugar glue and if necessary support with kitchen paper while it dries.

8 For the paddles, draw around the 2.5cm (1in) circle cutter, with the edible ink pen, on to the rice paper. Mark one straight edge on each paddle and cut out the shapes using a craft knife. Paint with the edible lustre spray in pearl, as this will help to shape the paddles, and secure these to each end of the lollipop stick with a little buttercream.

Man Overboard!

Oh dear ... it looks like a canoe has flipped over! The canoe in the background was made from blue paste; don't remove the centre circle and smooth the paste away from the centre with the rolling pin before cutting it out.

Swimming

Materials:

Modelling paste: flesh,
  brown

White sugarpaste,
  250g (8oz)

Piping gel

Edible ink pen in brown

Food colouring in blue

Sugar glue

Tools:

Marzipan/plastic spacers,
  1.3cm (½in) depth

Non-stick rolling pin

Circle cutter, 2.5cm (1in)

Fluted oval cutter,
  12.7cm (5in)

Craft knife

Mini ball tool

Mini scallop tool

Piping tube no. 3 or 4

Smoother

Small paintbrush

Instructions:

1 Knead a few drops of blue food colouring into the sugarpaste until it has marbled and cut out the base for your project using the 12.7cm (5in) fluted oval cutter. Put to one side.

2 For the head, use half a circle of flesh-coloured modelling paste and follow the instructions on page 7. Add on the eyebrows with the edible ink pen once the paste has dried. Make the ears, nose and mouth according to the instructions on page 7.

3 For the hair, roll three very small balls of paste into teardrop shapes and secure to the top of the head with sugar glue.

4 For the body, roll a quarter of a circle of flesh-coloured paste into a cone shape and place it below the head.

5 For each arm, use half a circle of flesh-coloured paste and follow the instructions on page 6, positioning these at the side of the head.

6 For the feet, use one-eighth of a circle of flesh-coloured paste for each foot, roll into an oval shape, flatten each slightly and secure away from the body, allowing for where the legs would be.

7 Colour the piping gel with blue food colouring and paint it liberally on to the surrounding fluted paste oval and over the swimmer's body.

Making a Splash

Only another twenty lengths of the pool to go and these two are neck and neck ... but which of our competitors has their eyes on the prize? Try varying the hair colour and facial expression on your swimmer; experiment with different coloured pastes and tools.

Synchronised Swimming

Materials:

Modelling paste in flesh

White sugarpaste, 250g (8oz)

Food colouring in blue

Piping gel, 2 heaped
  tablespoons (plus a little
  for gluing)

Tools:

Marzipan/plastic spacers,
  1.3cm (½in) depth

Non-stick rolling pin

Circle cutter, 2.5cm (1in)

Fluted oval cutter, 12.7cm (5in)

Smoother

Craft knife

Ball tool

Kitchen paper

Small paintbrush

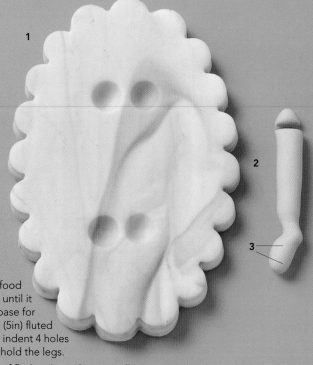

Instructions:

1 Knead a few drops of blue food
colouring into the sugarpaste until it
has marbled and cut out the base for
your project using the 12.7cm (5in) fluted
oval cutter. With the ball tool, indent 4 holes
into the paste oval; these will hold the legs.

2 For the legs, use one circle of flesh-coloured paste, roll into a sausage
shape 10cm (4in) long, cut in half and follow the modelling instructions
on page 6.

3 Bend the thinned ankle area to an 'L' shape for the foot, indent the
sole lightly with the ball tool to shape and repeat for the second leg.

4 Secure the legs into the holes with a little piping gel on the paste oval.
Support them with a piece of rolled-up kitchen paper and leave them to
dry thoroughly.

5 Remove the kitchen paper, colour some piping gel with blue food
colouring and paint it around the legs to look like water.

Vary the flesh tones on the swimmer's legs and make as
many pairs as you like until you have a full team.

Archery

Materials:

Modelling paste:
white, yellow, red,
blue, black, brown,
pale blue, flesh

White sugarpaste,
250g (8oz)

Wheat cereal
biscuits, x 4

Thin sugar sticks

Buttercream/frosting

Sugar glue

Edible ink pen in
brown

Edible lustre spray
in bronze

Tools:

Marzipan/plastic
spacers, 1.3cm
(½in) depth

Non-stick rolling pin

Fluted oval cutter,
12.7cm (5in)

Circle cutters, 1.3cm
(½in), 2.5cm (1in),
3cm (1⅛in), 4.5cm
(1¾in), 5.7cm
(2¼in), 7cm (2¾in)

Blossom plunger,
1cm (⅜in)

Smoother

Quilting tool/
stitching wheel

Craft knife

Cocktail stick

Scriber

Mini ball tool

Mini scallop tool

Piping tubes no. 3, 17

Kitchen paper

Small paintbrush

Instructions:

1 To make the base, roll out white sugarpaste, cut out an oval using the 12.7cm (5in) fluted oval cutter and put to one side.

2 To make the target, roll out some white modelling paste, cut out two circles using the 7cm (2¾in) cutter and then cut out a 5.7cm (2¼in) circle from one of them. Remove this smaller circle of paste and discard. Lay the remaining white ring on top of the 7cm (2¾in) paste circle.

3 Make a black ring in the same way using the 5.7cm (2¼in) and 4.5cm (1¾in) cutters.

4 Make a pale blue ring using the 4.5cm (1¾in) and 3cm (1⅛in) cutters.

5 Make a red ring using the 3cm (1⅛in) and 1.3cm (½in) cutters. Place the rings on the target as shown opposite.

6 Roll out a very small amount of yellow paste and cut out a circle using the 1.3cm (½in) cutter. Emboss the centre with piping tube no. 17 and place it inside the red circle. The rings of paste will be fresh enough to not require gluing. Leave the target to dry overnight. Use buttercream to glue the wheat cereal biscuits together in a stack on top of the white paste oval, and then glue the target in position leaning against the stacked biscuits.

7 For the legs, roll two circles of blue into a sausage shape approximately 14cm (5½in) long and follow the instructions on page 6. Bend it in half to make two legs and trim flat at the base. Use the quilting tool/stitching wheel to add a zip. Secure to the white base with a little buttercream and leave it to dry overnight.

8 For the body, take one and a half circles of blue paste and make it in the same way as for the footballer on page 8. Secure to the legs with sugar glue.

9 To make the arms, use one circle of blue paste and follow the instructions for the arms of the canoeist on page 31. Using sugar glue, secure one arm resting on the target, push a cocktail stick in to support it and rest the other arm on top of the target. Remove the cocktail stick when the arms have dried completely (use this hole to hold the sugar stick arrow later).

10 For the hands, take an eighth of a circle of flesh-coloured paste and model them, following the instructions on page 6. Secure in place with sugar glue.

11 Make an arm guard by rolling a pea-sized ball of black paste into an oval shape. Flatten it slightly and secure on to the arm with sugar glue. Make straps with tiny sausage shapes of black paste and secure to either side of the guard using sugar glue.

12 For the head, use half a circle of flesh-coloured paste and follow the instructions on page 7. Make the eyes in the same way as for the gymnast on page 23. Add hair by rolling out some brown paste, and follow the instructions for the footballer's hair on page 9.

13 For the hat, roll out red paste and cut out a circle with the 2.5cm (1in) cutter. Lightly mark on a semi-circle using the same cutter to make the peak. Use the mini ball tool to mark on a circle in the crown of the hat and add a very tiny ball of red paste. Secure to the head with sugar glue.

14 To make the arrow, colour a sugar stick with edible lustre spray in bronze and allow to dry. Roll three very tiny balls of red paste into teardrop shapes and secure to the stick for feathers. Insert the arrow into the hole made earlier by the cocktail stick. Support underneath with kitchen paper until everything is completely dry.

Bullseye!

Desperate to add another string to his bow, this archer won't rest until he hits his target spot on.

Golf

Tools:

Marzipan/plastic spacers,
   1.3cm (½in) depth

Non-stick rolling pin

Fluted oval cutter, 12.7cm (5in)

Circle cutter, 2.5cm (1in)

Blossom plunger, 1cm (⅜in)

Craft knife

Smoother

Small scissors

Mini ball tool

Scriber

Blade tool

Small paintbrush

Materials:

Modelling paste: dark
   orange, white, brown

White sugarpaste, 250g (8oz)

Edible ink pen in black
   and brown

Edible lustre spray in green
   and silver

Lollipop stick

Sugar glue

Instructions:

1 Roll out the white sugarpaste between the spacers and cut out an oval using the 12.7cm (5in) fluted oval cutter. Indent a hole into the paste oval with the mini ball tool (for the golf hole), spray with the edible lustre spray in green and leave to dry.

2 For the legs, use two circles of brown paste and follow the modelling instructions on page 6. Roll into a sausage shape to a length of 12.7cm (5in) and bend it in half (so that your golfer can kneel). Create a waist by bending the paste upwards slightly at one end, pinch the knees to a point for definition and secure to the oval shape with sugar glue.

3 To make each shoe, roll an eighth of a white paste circle into an oval, flatten slightly and add the heel detail using the blade tool. Secure a shoe under each leg with sugar glue and leave to dry overnight.

4 For the upper body, use one circle of white paste and follow the instructions on page 8 for making the footballer's shirt.

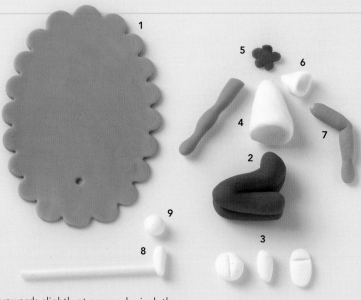

5 For the head and nose, use half a circle of dark orange paste and follow the instructions on page 7. Roll out some brown paste for the hair, cut out a shape using the 1cm (⅜in) blossom plunger and attach to the head with sugar glue. Once the paste is dry, use the edible ink pen to draw on eyes and eyebrows (there is no need to draw a mouth as this will be covered by the golfer's hands).

6 For the sleeves, use an eighth of a circle of white paste and follow the instructions to make the footballer's shirt sleeves on page 9.

7 To make each arm, use half a circle of dark orange paste and follow the instructions on page 6. Secure them into the shirt sleeves with sugar glue and bend them into position with the hands covering the golfer's mouth in anguish!

8 For the golf club, cut a lollipop stick to a length of 7.5cm (3in) and roll a pea-sized ball of white paste into an oval shape. Attach the paste oval to the lollipop stick with a little sugar glue. Leave to dry and then paint in silver edible lustre spray.

9 Roll a very tiny ball of white paste for the golf ball and place it somewhere on the green fluted oval.

Hole in One

It's up to you – will it be a hit or a miss for your golfer? Simply position the golf ball wherever you choose on the grassy oval to decide his fate.

Tennis

Materials:

Modelling paste: white, flesh, pale brown, black, yellow

White sugarpaste, 250g (8oz)

Rice paper

Edible ink pen in black

Buttercream/frosting

Sugar glue

Lollipop stick

Edible lustre spray in green

Tools:

Marzipan/plastic spacers 1.3cm (½in) depth

Non-stick rolling pin

Fluted oval cutter, 12.7cm (5in)

Circle cutter, 2.5cm (1in)

Square cutter, 4cm (1½in)

Smoother

Scriber

Mini ball tool

Mini scallop tool

Cutting wheel

Craft knife

Leaf veining tool

Small scissors

Ruler

Food bag

Kitchen paper

Piping tube no. 4

Small paintbrush

Instructions:

1 Roll out white sugarpaste between the spacers and cut out the fluted oval shape using the 12.7cm (5in) cutter. Spray with green edible lustre spray and leave to dry.

2 For the legs, use two circles of flesh-coloured paste, roll them into a sausage shape 12.7cm (5in) long and follow the instructions on page 6. Mark on the knee joints with the mini ball tool.

3 Roll out white modelling paste quite thinly and cut out three squares with the 4cm (1½in) cutter. Store two in the food bag. Cut one square into quarters and use one quarter for each of the socks; secure at the base of each leg with sugar glue. Place the other two quarters back into the food bag.

4 For the skirt, take the white squares out of the food bag and place one above the knees at the back of the legs and the other at the front. Trim to fit neatly and secure to the legs with sugar glue. Bend the legs at the knee and position your tennis player on the green oval base.

5 Make each shoe by rolling an eighth of a white circle into an oval, flatten slightly and run a cutting wheel around its edge to look like a sole.

Tennis racket template (actual size)

6 For the vest, use two white circles of paste and follow the instructions on page 10 for the basketball player's vest. Use flesh-coloured paste for the chest.

7 For the arms, use half a circle of flesh-coloured paste and follow the modelling instructions on page 6. Roll to a sausage shape, 9.5cm (3¾in) long and secure to the body in an action pose, with one hand raised to her face and the other nearer the base. Use some kitchen paper to support the arms as the model dries.

8 Take your leftover squares out of the food bag, cut them into strips to make wrist bands and secure in place with sugar glue.

9 For the head use half a circle of flesh-coloured paste and follow the instructions on page 7. Model the nose as on page 7 and use the piping tube to mark on the eyes.

10 For the hair and fringe, roll out some pale brown paste and cut out a 2.5cm (1in) circle with the cutter. Re-cut to remove an oval of paste from the circle and add texture to both pieces with the leaf veining tool. Secure the larger piece to the head with sugar glue. Add a strip of white leftover paste for a head band and secure the fringe over the top of it with sugar glue. Add bunches to the sides of the head made from teardrop shapes of pale brown paste. Texture with the leaf veining tool.

Game, Set, Match!
The perfect cake topper to adorn a summer cake come Wimbledon season! Serve alongside your strawberries and cream!

11 To make the tennis racket, use the template to draw with the black edible ink pen on the rice paper, cut around the shape and use a ruler to mark on lots of horizontal and vertical lines. Cut a lollipop stick to a length of 5cm (2in), add a strip of black paste for the handle and secure the rice paper with a little buttercream. Secure the tennis racket into the player's hand with a little buttercream, or leave it resting by her side.

12 Roll a little yellow paste into a ball for a tennis ball and place at the player's side.

Show Jumping

Materials:

Modelling paste:
brown 250g (8oz),
black, red,
white, flesh

Rice paper

Chocolate fingers

Sugar glue

Edible lustre spray
in silver

Liquorice strand

Wheat cereal biscuits,
x 2

Buttercream/frosting

Tools:

Marzipan/plastic
spacers, 1.3cm
(½in) depth

Non-stick rolling pin

Circle cutter, 2.5cm
(1in)

Oval cutter, 3cm
(1¼in)

Leaf veining tool

Mini scallop tool

Cocktail stick

Ball tool/mini ball tool

Small paintbrush

Piping tubes no. 4, 17

Smoother

Scriber

Craft knife

Cutting wheel

Tweezers

Food bag

Instructions

1 Position and secure one wheat
cereal biscuit on top of the other with
buttercream to make the jump. Cut the
chocolate fingers to size and arrange
around the front of the jump for a fence.

2 For the horse, roll 200g (7oz) of brown
paste into a pear shape, elongate the
narrow end using your fingers to make a
neck and the horse's nose.

3 Mark the eye sockets and nostrils with
the mini ball tool. Mark a mouth with a
craft knife and a smile at each corner with
the leaf veining tool. Secure the horse
with buttercream over the wheat jump,
and leave to dry overnight.

4 For the horse's legs take one circle of
brown paste and roll it into a sausage
shape 10cm (4in) long. Divide it in half,
make ankles by using your finger and
flatten the end on the work surface to
make a hoof on each. Secure to the body
with sugar glue at the shoulders, drape
over the jump and push firmly to secure.
No rear legs are made.

5 To make the saddle, take a strand of
liquorice and wrap it around the horse's
body, securing with buttercream. Roll
out some black paste, not too thinly, and
cut out three 3cm (1¼in) ovals. Make the
saddle out of these three ovals and attach
them to the horse with sugar glue.

6 Take some rolled-out black paste and
use a cutting wheel to cut strips for the

bridle. Make the nose band slightly thicker. Cut out the bit using the piping tubes, and secure to the head with sugar glue, using the photograph as a guide. Make some reins too but do not attach yet and store in a food bag.

7 For each of the horse's ears, roll a pea-sized ball of paste into a triangle and indent with the flat end of a leaf veining tool. For the mane, tail, forelock and rider's hair, follow the instructions for the swimmer's hair on page 32 using brown paste.

8 For the horse's eyes, roll out some brown paste, not too thinly, and use a piping tube no. 17 to cut out a circle. Divide it in half, roll each half into a ball, secure in each socket and indent with the mini ball tool. Roll a very small ball of black paste and cut it in half for each pupil. Use sugar glue to attach the pupils to the brown paste.

9 To make each jodhpur leg, roll one circle of white paste into a sausage shape 6.5cm 2(½in) long, tapered at each end for the knees. Secure the legs to the front of the saddle, one on each side.

10 For the boots, roll one circle of black paste into a sausage shape 5cm (2in) long and cut it in half, to make two boots. Bend each one into an 'L' shape and mark on a sole using the cutting wheel. Indent the top of each boot with the ball tool, insert the leg slightly inside each boot and secure with sugar glue on the saddle. Use cocktail sticks to hold them in place until they are dry.

11 For the red jacket (body), use one circle of red paste and make it in the same way as for the footballer on page 8. Secure to the jodhpurs with sugar glue.

12 For the arms, use half a circle of red paste and follow the instructions for the canoeist's arms on page 31 without cutting away at the shoulder or adding texture.

13 For the head, use one circle of flesh-coloured paste and follow the modelling instructions on page 7. Cut the head in half in order for the hat to fit (use the bottom half). Make the nose and mouth as on page 7.

14 For the hat, roll one black circle of paste into a ball and cut it in half. Roll out the remaining paste, cut out a 2.5cm (1in) circle and cut this in half for the brim. Secure the brim to the hat and the hat to the head with sugar glue.

15 Make the hands using black paste as on page 6.

16 To make stirrups, cut out a small triangle of rice paper and remove another small triangle shape from its centre using a craft knife. Paint the shape with a little edible lustre spray in silver, cut it in half and use tweezers to push it into the side of each boot. Finally attach the reins to the horse's bridle and into the rider's hands.

Ice Skating

Materials:

Modelling paste: lilac, beige, black, white

White sugarpaste, 250g (8oz)

Rice paper

Edible ink pen in black or blue

Edible lustre spray in blue and pearl

Edible dust in red

Sugar glue

Buttercream/frosting

Tools:

Marzipan/plastic spacers, 1.3cm (½in) depth

Non-stick rolling pin

Oval cutter, 12.7cm (5in)

Circle cutter, 2.5cm (1in)

Smoother

Round/wavy cutter, 4.5cm (1¾in)

Piping tube no. 3 or 4

Bulbous cone tool

Kitchen paper

Foam pad

Small paintbrush

Craft knife

Tweezers

Leaf veining tool

Scriber or cocktail stick

Mini ball tool

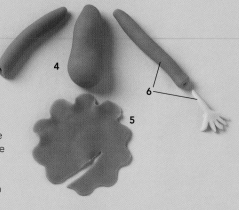

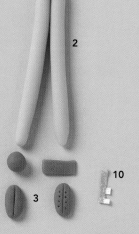

Instructions:

1 For the base, roll out the white sugarpaste between the spacers and cut out two oval shapes using the 12.7cm (5in) cutter. Spray one with edible pearl lustre and use a little buttercream to stick one on top of the other. Secure a folded sheet of rice paper (for the edge of the ice rink) to the oval with a little buttercream. Use a ball of paste to hold it in place until the buttercream has dried.

2 For the legs, use one circle of beige paste rolled into a sausage shape 15cm (6in) long. Follow the instructions for modelling on page 6 and fold in half to make two legs.

3 For the boots, roll a pea-sized ball of lilac paste into an oval shape for each one. Flatten it slightly at the top and bottom. Use a craft knife to mark on a line down the centre-top and bottom and a scriber to mark on four small holes either side of the line, for the bootlace eyelets. Roll out some lilac paste and cut out a small rectangle for each boot, securing them directly above each boot, wrapped around each leg at the ankle. Add in some more eyelets to these rectangles on each boot.

4 For the body, use one circle of lilac paste rolled into an oval (following the instructions on page 6) and secure above the legs with sugar glue.

5 For the skater's skirt, thinly roll out one fluted circle of lilac paste using the 4.5cm (1¾in) wavy cutter and, using a bulbous cone tool, place it on the soft foam pad edge and create undulations on the skirt's edge by rocking the large part of the tool back and forth around the edge of the paste circle. Apply pressure and rock the tool to the left, then to the right, working on a small area at a time. Make a cut in the skirt as shown and secure with sugar glue around the body.

6 For each arm, use half a circle of lilac paste and follow the instructions for modelling on page 6. Secure each one to the body with sugar glue. Make the hands out of beige paste following the instructions on pages 6–7 and attach to the arms.

7 For the head, use half a circle of beige paste and follow the instructions on page 7. Make the nose as on page 7 also. Make the eyes as for the footballer on page 9 or draw them on with an edible ink pen, once the paste has fully dried. Mark the mouth with the mini ball tool. Add rosy cheeks with the edible red dust.

8 For the hair, roll black paste into large teardrop shapes and mark on some texture with a leaf veining tool before securing on to the head with sugar glue.

9 When everything has dried, use some edible lustre spray in blue, sprayed into the can lid and painted on with a paintbrush, to paint a design of your choice on to the dress and skirt.

10 To make the blades for the boots cut out two small 'f' shapes from the rice paper and paint with the edible blue lustre. When they are dry, use tweezers to insert them into the slit on the underside of each boot (marked on in step 3).

Get Your Skates On!

For a quick and simple take on this project, just make the ice skates, in any colour you like, and position them on a white iced cake. Great for someone special who loves this graceful sport.

Skiing

Materials:

Modelling paste: blue, red, black, white, flesh

Rice paper

Edible ink pen (any colour)

Sugar glue

Edible red dust

Tools:

Marzipan/plastic spacers, 1.3cm (½in) depth

Non-stick rolling pin

Circle cutter, 2.5cm (1in)

Square cutter, 4cm (1½in)

Smoother

Small paintbrush

Small drinking straws x 2

Craft knife

Scriber

Quilting tool/stitching wheel or cocktail stick

Ball tool

Mini ball tool

Small scissors

Cutting wheel

Piping tube no. 3 or 4, 17

Kitchen paper

Instructions:

1 Make a pair of skis out of rice paper. Using an edible ink pen, draw two rectangles 9cm x 1cm (3½in x ½in) on to the rice paper and cut out with the scissors. Cut one end of each ski into a point and lightly curl the ends by pulling the paper through between closed scissors and our thumb.

2 For each leg and boot use one and a half circles of blue paste and roll to a length of 7.5cm (3in). Texture the outer side of each leg, from top to bottom, with a quilting tool/stitching wheel or cocktail stick, bend at the knee and heel, and model a foot at the end of each leg.

3 Cut out two circles of blue paste for the body and roll into a pear shape, marking on a zip with the cutting wheel. Push a thumb up into the wide end of the pear to create a hollow. Secure on to the tops of the legs with sugar glue.

4 Use a pea-sized ball of blue paste for the collar, roll into a ball and flatten slightly. Mark on some vertical lines on the outer edge with the cutting wheel and secure to the top of the body with sugar glue.

5 For the head, use half a circle of flesh-coloured paste and add on a nose as on page 7. For the scarf, roll out some red paste, cut out a square using the 4cm (1½in) cutter and cut off a triangle (see opposite). Position it under the nose and add movement by twisting it slightly.

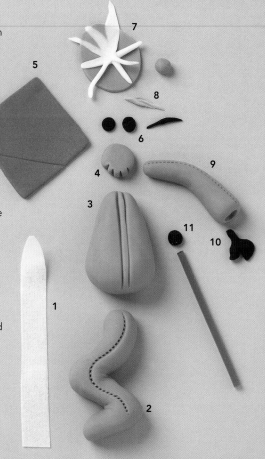

6 Make the sunglasses with black paste as for the windsurfer on page 27. Add two thin sausage shapes of paste either side of the head to make the glasses' arms.

7 For the hat, roll out some blue paste thinly. Roll four thin sausage shapes of white paste and place these across each other, like an asterisk on the blue paste. Use a rolling pin to blend the colours together, then cut out a circle using the 2.5 cm (1in) cutter. Secure to the top of the head with sugar glue. Roll a tiny amount of blue paste into a ball to make the bobble and secure to the hat with sugar glue.

8 For the hair, follow the instructions for the swimmers on page 32.

9 For the arms, use one circle of blue paste, roll into a sausage shape 10cm (4in) long and follow the instructions on page 6. Cut it in half to make two arms, indent at one end with the ball tool (this is where the hands will go) and add stitch detail as for the legs. Secure to the body with sugar glue.

10 For the gloves, take a little black paste and model mitten shapes following the directions on pages 6–7. Attach them to the arms with sugar glue and wrap them around each small drinking straw (ski pole).

11 Add a small black ball of paste to the top of each ski pole. Use the no.17 piping tube as a size guide and secure with sugar glue. Give your skier rosy cheeks using a little edible red dust and a small paintbrush.

Hit the Slopes
Whoops! This fun alternative was made by spraying a ball of white sugar paste with edible lustre spray in pearl, with the boots and skis sticking out. It's a human snowball!

Acknowledgements

I would like to thank the whole team at Search Press for all their hard work and help; with special thanks to Alison for her editing skills, to Marrianne and Juan for bringing the paste figures to life and to Paul for his wonderful photography. Also, thank you to Pat and Shailesh at Knightsbridge Pme Ltd for their help with both edibles and equipment for all the projects in this book. Lastly, a special thanks to Steph and Glen for assisting their mum with speedy typing when I needed it the most! And to Steve for coping with me! Thank you all!

You are invited to visit the
author's website
www.creativecakecompany.com

Publisher's Note

If you would like more information about baking and sugarcraft, try:
Celebration Cake Pops by Paula MacLeod, Search Press, 2011 or *Sugar Birds,* 2011, *Sugar Fairies,* 2010 or *Sugar Animals,* 2009 all by Frances McNaughton, Search Press, in the Twenty to Make series.